Hidden Heritage

Written by Lynette Evans
Photography by Ted Wood

Mexico

Kin's father and grandfather have taught him to respect many of the traditional Maya ways. However, it is not until Kin explores some ancient Maya ruins near his home that his family's traditions suddenly come alive.

respect to place a high value on something

Contents

Hidden Heritage

When Kin turned twelve, he began to help his father make hunting arrows and clay figures to sell to tourists. The tourists come each day to see the great pyramids on the edge of town. They buy the crafts Kin's father makes in the traditional Maya way.

Kin says that the clay comes from a special place in the jungle. When the clay is dry, Kin will help bake the figures in the hot coals of a fire.

Now Kin's father wants him to learn the customs of his Maya ancestors. "The arrows and clay figures are part of our past," Kin's father tells him. "It's important to keep our aim true, even if the world has changed."

custom   a special way of doing things

Kin lives with his family in the town of Palenque (*pah LANE kay*), Mexico. He is a Lacando'n Indian boy, and his people have lived in this part of Mexico for hundreds of years.

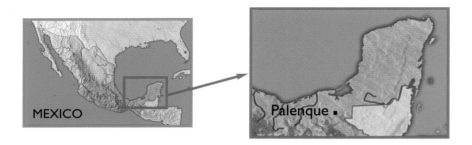

Until now, Kin has not been very interested in the old Maya ways. When his grandfather speaks to him in the Maya language, Kin understands, but he prefers to speak Spanish, like most people in Mexico.

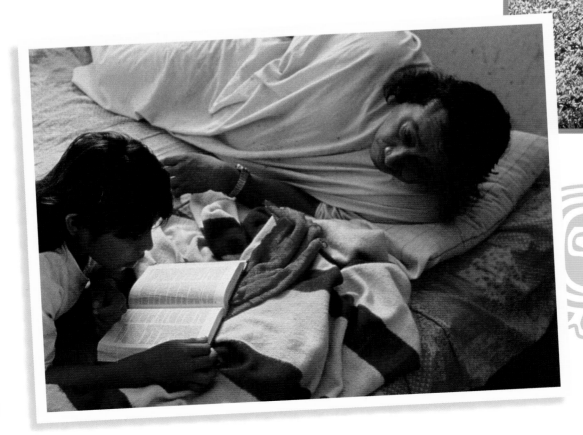

Like the Lacando'n Indians who once roamed the forests of Palenque, Kin has long hair. He is not allowed to cut it short. How would you feel about this?

One evening, Kin's grandfather showed him a book about the pyramids and a Maya king named Pacal. Kin learned that Pacal's tomb was in the pyramid ruins. That was when Kin decided it was time he went exploring!

tomb   a place in which a dead body is kept

The pyramids are so tall that Kin has to bend his head all the way back to see the tops. Some are half-hidden by jungle. Others have steps like long ladders leading up the sides. Kin starts to climb one of the tallest pyramids. It is hard work going up the steep steps in the hot sun, but Kin makes it to the top.

Kin read that it took the Maya hundreds of years to build the pyramids with stones they cut from solid rock and carried through the jungle.

Kin remembers his grandfather telling him that the ancient Maya were one of the first peoples to develop their own written language.

Kin wanders through the ruins. He twists and turns through a maze of stairways and underground passages. He stops to look at carvings with picture writing and symbols.

symbol   an object that stands for something else

Kin has fun as he searches for Pacal's tomb.
He jumps over the gaps in the old stone walls.

Then Kin climbs a tall pyramid in the center
of a plaza. He counts the steps as he goes up.

plaza   an open area in the middle of buildings

Deep inside the pyramid, down a long, dark tunnel and some slippery stone steps, Kin finds the tomb of Pacal.

Pacal was twelve years old when he became king. He ruled for 67 years and built many pyramids. What kind of person do you think Pacal must have been?

On the way home, Kin feels lonely and a little sad. He wishes he could travel back in time to meet Pacal and the amazing Maya who built the pyramids. Then Kin's father stops at a huge statue in the center of town. Kin has seen it many times, but now he recognizes it as the face of Pacal.

Suddenly, Kin understands that although he and Pacal live in worlds that are hundreds of years apart, they are still brothers. The same Maya blood runs through their veins. Kin feels proud to be Maya. His ancestors no longer seem so far away. Now, for the very first time, Kin knows how it feels to be a king!

Many towns have statues and monuments that help people remember people and events from the past. What famous faces and places are commemorated where you live?

commemorate   to serve as a reminder of

Did You Know?

Jaguars are the largest, most powerful wild cats in the western part of the world. Many jaguars once roamed the forests and jungles of Mexico and nearby lands. The jaguar was a symbol of strength and courage to the ancient Maya.

The Maya people were skilled farmers. They dug canals to drain the soil and grew crops, such as maize, that fed many people.

Buildings were often erected on poles, and people used palm leaves or grass to thatch the roofs.

13

Explore Mexico

Mexico is a large country in Latin America. There are many active volcanoes among the snowcapped mountain ranges that crisscross the land. The mountains surround high plateaus and deep canyons. Great deserts stretch across the northwest, and thick, tropical rainforests grow in the south. Mexico is located on the Pacific Ring of Fire and is often shaken by earthquakes.

Mountain lions and deer live high in the mountains of Mexico. Coyotes, prairie dogs, and rattlesnakes are found in the deserts, and many kinds of colorful birds and other animals live in the forests.

In volcanic areas, hardy plants, such as cactuses, grow on the volcanic rocks.

Pacific Ring of Fire   the area around the Pacific Ocean where 75 percent of the world's volcanoes are found

Mexico City is the capital of Mexico. The city is surrounded by mountains.

On the Go!

Which country is the world's largest Spanish-speaking country?
Go to page 17

Who was the child code breaker of ancient Maya picture writing?
Go to page 21

What words in English first came from Mexico?
Go to page 23

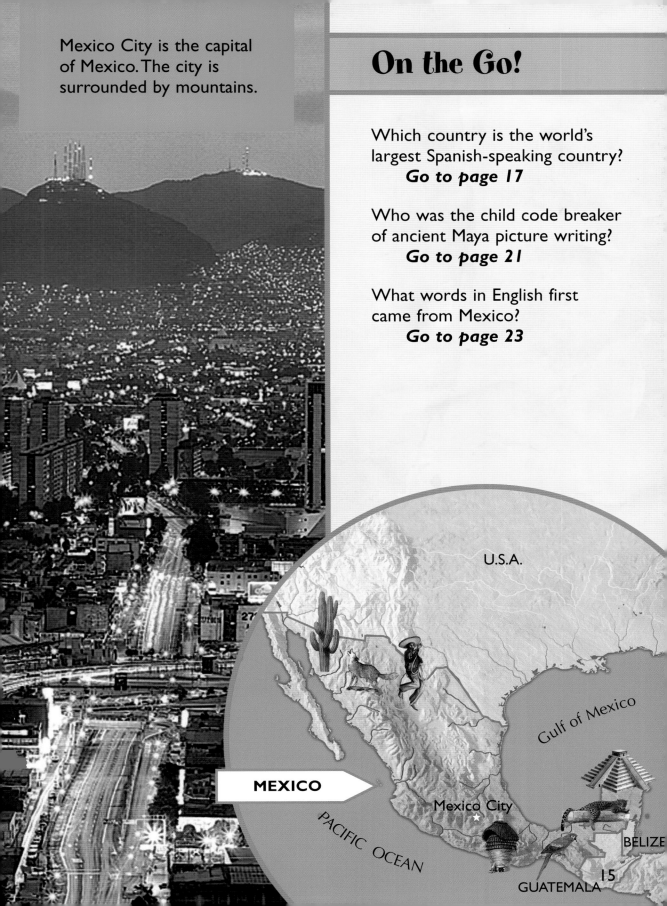

U.S.A.

Gulf of Mexico

MEXICO

Mexico City

PACIFIC OCEAN

BELIZE

GUATEMALA

15

Faces and Places

People have lived in Mexico for thousands of years. Long ago, the Maya and Aztec Indians built large cities and ruled powerful empires there. Later, the Spanish came. They controlled Mexico for almost 300 years. Although Spanish rule of Mexico ended in 1821, the Spanish culture remains strong to this day.

Mexico now has many bustling cities and is home to more than 100 million people. Most are proud of their Indian heritage and keep the customs of old times alive in the colors, tastes, and celebrations of everyday life.

Hola = **Hello**

Sunday is a day off work for most Mexicans. Families and friends often picnic in the park or enjoy a game of soccer.

heritage   valuable traditions handed down from the past

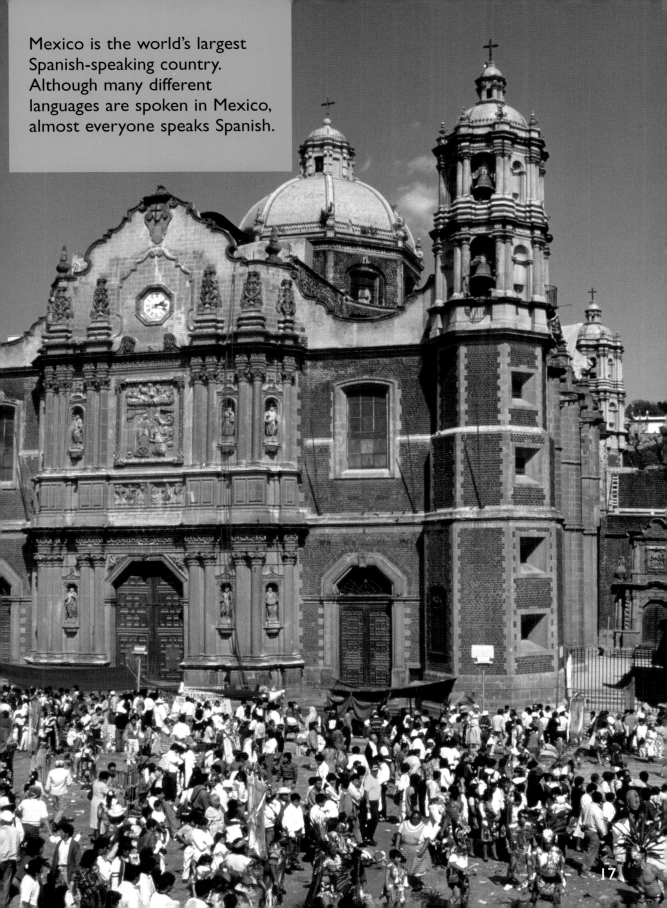

Mexico is the world's largest Spanish-speaking country. Although many different languages are spoken in Mexico, almost everyone speaks Spanish.

17

A Living History

Mexico is home to the oldest monuments in all of the Americas. Thousands of years ago, the peaceful Maya people built cities, pyramids, palaces, and temples throughout the land. They did this with simple tools of sharp stone and wood. They made beautiful, painted pottery, carved jade into jewelry, and wove colorful cotton clothing.

The Maya civilization ended by the year 900. No one knows why. All that remains of the great cities are the ruins. However, many modern Maya today still follow the traditional ways.

Today, there are more than six million modern Maya living in rural areas of Mexico, Guatemala, and Belize. They work hard to keep their ancient culture alive.

Did You Know?

The Maya were clever astronomers. They built observatories and plotted the movements of the Sun, Moon, and planets. They developed one of the world's earliest accurate calendars.

The Maya developed a system of writing made up of picture-symbols called glyphs (below). They kept records on large stone monuments called steles (*STEE leez*) and made books from the bark of fig trees.

Almost all the ancient Maya books were destroyed long ago. Why is it important to keep things from the past safe for the future?

Pieces of the Puzzle

Tourists from all over the world come to explore and admire the ancient ruins in Mexico. These sites also attract **archaeologists**, who come from near and far to search for clues that will help piece together a picture of the past. It has taken many years of hard work for people to uncover the lost culture of the Maya. Today, scientists use high-tech methods to find ancient Maya treasures both underground and underwater.

archaeologist a person who digs up old objects to learn about the past

Huge underground pools of fresh water called cenotes (*seh NO teez*) were an important source of water for the Maya. Today, underwater archaeologists explore these for new clues.

Kid Code Breaker

David Stuart was eight years old when he began drawing the glyphs that the ancient Maya used to record events in their lives. These were carved on great stone slabs or painted on murals. By drawing and studying the glyphs, David figured out what many of them meant. By the time he was twelve, he could read glyphs in only hours, while it took most scholars years to break the codes!

David Stuart as a child

David Stuart as an adult

Beyond Borders

Many of the colors, flavors, designs, and traditions of Mexico have found their way into the homes and everyday lives of people in many parts of the world.

Maize

When the Spanish conquered Mexico, they were hoping to find gold and silver to send back to Spain. Perhaps of more lasting value were the new foods they found. Maize, or corn, first came from Mexico.

Chocolate

People in Europe didn't know how good chocolate was until this new taste treat was brought back from Mexico. For years, the Maya and Aztec Indians had harvested the beans of the cacao tree to make chocolate.

Fun and Games

Piñatas are a popular party treat that first came from Mexico. These star-shaped containers are usually filled with candy, fruit, or toys. Children the world over enjoy breaking open a piñata with a stick.

Many words that we use in English first came from Mexico. Can you imagine why these words were invented in Mexico: *canyon, lasso, patio, rodeo, stampede*?

Hot Chili Peppers

Mexican food is famous for its hot, spicy taste. All over the world, Mexican chili peppers are now used to flavor food. There are many different kinds of chili peppers, and some are almost too hot to handle!

What Do You Think?

1. How do you think tourism helps keep the customs and traditions of the past alive in today's modern world?

2. When Kin explored the ruins, what do you think it was that made him most proud to be Mayan?

How did exploring the ruins help Kin to respect the traditions of the past and to value his Maya heritage?

Index